926 Raindrops

Gift of the Wild

Gloria Straube

Dedication

For 926F –

My love for you will live forever

Acknowledgment

I would like to express my special thanks of gratitude to Dr. Jane Goodall and Mr. Rick McIntyre.

"I feel it's really important to reach the heart, because people have got to change from within. They've got to change because they want to change. And if you batter at them and try to blind them with science, they don't want to listen to you. But if you can quietly tell a story, then you may reach the heart. And that's when people change."

-Dr. Jane Goodall, Primatologist

"This black wolf is the alpha female of the Lamar Canyon Pack. She is the daughter of the most famous wolf in the world, 832F. Consider yourself rewarded."

-Rick McIntyre, NPS Wolf Interpreter (Ret.), Author

Contents

About the Author

Gloria Straube is devoted to giving her readers a story filled with a nature-inspired wanderlust for all things wild, entangled with fate and a twist of true love.

In honor of the restoration of wolves back into Yellowstone National Park in 1995, Gloria has become a passionate advocate for better protection for the wolves and grizzly bears that call the Greater Yellowstone Ecosystem home. The Greater Yellowstone Ecosystem (GYE) is one of the last remaining large, nearly intact ecosystems located within the Northern Rocky Mountains. She has been involved with wolf issues and wolf organizations for over ten years. Gloria is committed to using her voice for these voiceless animals in the constant battle for better protection and coexistence. A lifetime observer of nature, she spends most of her free time studying the behavior of wolves and grizzly bears in the wild, quietly earning herself a coveted ethology background. Through her observations and personal stories, Gloria hopes to better inform the public on understanding the full importance of top predators to the ecosystem.

Gloria has a Bachelor of Science (B.S) degree from Emerson College.

She is happily married to Andy and has three young sons: Bennett, Luke, and Harrison.

Tadpoles and Rain

I grew up in Key West, Florida. The island of Key West is about 4 miles long and 1 mile wide, with a total land area of 4.2 square miles. It lies at the southernmost end of U.S. Route 1, the longest north-south road in the United States. The southernmost point in the continental United States ending at mile marker one. I grew up with a challenging background, not having a normal childhood like most kids. One thing you learn early on when you are exposed to a millenarian restorationist Christian denomination group with nontrinitarian beliefs distinct from mainstream Christianity is that true paradise seems much farther away. The self does not exist. You have to deny yourself. Psychologically, self-denial is unhealthy. And no, it's not just about being humble. It goes above and beyond that. As a child, all those little things that could make you feel worthwhile, valuable, and important are taken away one by one. Celebrating your birthday is to put yourself forward as if it were almost narcissistic to celebrate the day of your birth. A child with a strong denial of self will have a hard time accomplishing anything of consequence in life. In the end, because the denial of self is unnatural, the child who is taught to deny himself or herself will feel diminished and non-existent. Cognitive dissonance is the conflict that happens in your brain when facts and beliefs do not match. Extended exposure to cognitive dissonance can induce an emotional reaction that may grow more uncontrollably over time. Not having a normal childhood, I knew I was different.

I longed for the petite slivers of happiness. Most of the time, life seemed like nothing but a prison cell. During thunderstorms, I would be standing out on the streets when the other kids would sit at home, horrified by the lightning that could fall upon them. The clouds would turn gray and frightening, but I would stand there fearless, and look forward to dancing in the rain. With the rain, I felt like I had somehow absconded from the iron cage in which I was held captive. My mind would be at peace, as with the raindrops, the sadness, and feelings of being trapped would wash away. I would stand there without knowing that I had been having the best time of my life.

With the rain, the thoughts that I had buried deep down in my heart would sway back up to my head, constantly prompting me about the things that I had lacked. They were the ceaseless souvenirs of everything I had desired and planned to do yet failed to chase. The rain helped cleanse my sadness and helped me feel connected to everything I was supposed to connect to. I had dreams that I thought I could not achieve, I had ambitions that I believed unattainable, and I had expectations from my future that I believed would turn into despairs and miseries. And thereby, I pretended. I pretended everything was going exactly as planned and anticipated. For most kids, the divine purposes of their existence and lives are their ambitions, the things they have obsessed over. For me, it was only isolation and no inspiration to be found anywhere nearby.

My family had loved me unconditionally and without limits, but I knew not how to control the way I felt. It seemed like a void was yet to be filled, but I had no idea how it would be filled. It was like my heart had been impaired beyond any sort of amendment. Since the beginning, I had been different from the kids of my age – what had terrified them had given me pleasure. Subsequently, I was typically found alone, either playing in the rain or gazing at the exquisiteness that nature had to offer.

While the other kids would play with cats, I had developed a profound admiration for tadpoles. I had loved to rescue them following the rains, as they struggled to sustain themselves in this cruel world. The tadpoles were the commencement of the love I hold for animals. With the tadpoles, I would think about everything I had always wanted to be. And at that moment, I would know it was all attainable. I would be ensured nothing in this world was impossible. And thereby, I would hold on. The surrounding nature has always been the best thing to ever happen to me, everything that existed to make life glorious. I was sure that if one thing acts as the villain, there will be another thing that acts against it. There will always be a hero to save the day. I would hold on to the things that made life colorful for me, despite the endless and reckless shades of gray and blue that would parade over my head.

I would keep the tadpoles in buckets filled with water, and I would raise them in my backyard dollhouse. I would feed them, ensuring they do not fall prey to another animal foraging for its own survival. How pretty and ingenious they appeared as I stared at them; it made my eyes watery. In them, I observed the purity lacking in the whole wide world. And in them, I encountered the beauty taken away from me. With the tadpoles, I would feel like a normal child. With them, I could think of myself as an ordinary child who was determined to play more and think less about the wickedness and atrocities of life.

Though I held no such proportions of memories, I knew that life was still worth all of it – a part of me assured me that it was. I knew that I understood the traumas of loneliness, and I knew that I had been desolate almost all my childhood life. Sometimes, I was captivated with the inner sadness and thought maybe I would let my dreams slip away from my hands. But there were also times when I knew there was too much that I would miss out on. There were also times when I knew that life still had so much to show me, and I felt it was going to be something special. So, I would tell myself that the risk was too much to be taken, and if the odds were in my favor, it would positively be a shame to give it all up. When my mind struggled vigorously to go to the dark side, I would tell myself, "Not today."

Growing up in Key West, I had been blessed in two ways that held significant magnitude in my life. I had not made many pleasurable memories, but how I danced in the rain and played with the tadpoles made up most of my childhood. And I never felt remorseful for it; I never regretted being introverted. I was delighted with myself, and that was the only thing that mattered to me. I was satisfied with the friends I had – the tadpoles – because with them came no emotional or mental hurt whatsoever.

As the tadpoles grew and it was time for them to be free, I would take them to the nearby ponds that awaited me. Key West had been close to my heart since the start due to the ocean. The rain had been captivating and magical for me, while the ocean presented itself as the freedom to my thoughts and adverse emotions. I would sit there, all alone with my thoughts, as I would let my tadpoles, by now baby frogs, hop away to never return. I would sit there, thinking about becoming a mermaid. I would imagine myself as a blonde with a turquoise tail attached to my waist instead of my legs. As the tadpoles, by now frogs, would go far away from me, I would sit there, and I would be reminded of how nothing in life stays. I had always known the tadpoles would grow into frogs, and they would have to be set out in the wild, where they had always belonged. They were there for a short time, yet they had made my life better in ways that no one else could.

One particular song my grandparents had sung back at their home would be on my mind and lips. It was probably one of a few songs I had learned the lyrics to. My grandparents always played music, singing that song over and over. It was one of the memories that I had cherished in my life. It was one of the few and easily countable memories I had made in my childhood. And as I would sit there at the beach on the sand that drew my hands in my brain would jog my memory to the mirth and the still audible laughter. The song was 'Raindrops keep fallin' on my head' by R. J. Thomas. And knowing that they had tried their level best to see a smile on

my face, I would remember them, and I would sing to
myself:

Raindrops keep falling on my head

But that doesn't mean my eyes

Will soon be turning red

Crying's not for me cause,

I'm never gonna stop the rain

By complaining,

Because I'm free

Nothings worrying me

It won't be long

Till happiness

Steps up to greet me

Raindrops keep falling on my head

Singing that song, I would long to feel the ocean. I had
learned how to swim without anyone else's help. I would run
off into the wide and perpetual ocean, knowing that there
would be no one to stop me or judge me. I pretended to be

whatever I wanted to be. After some time, when I would be exhausted, I would return to the shore and sit with my legs stretched out. The waves would crash on my toes, and for me, that moment elaborated harmony. At that moment, I knew that I was free to be a child. I knew that I did not have to pretend anymore. I knew that life had been tough for me, but it did not have to stay that way. So, I held on to the hope of a better future and let the waves wash away all my pains. As I would sit there, I would be reminded of the fact that we come alone into this lonesome world, and we live our lives in loneliness to pass on. I was recalled that life is but a wandering shadow, a wretched melodrama. It excites and agonizes with a few of its moments upon the stage, and then is never again heard from. It is but a narrative drafted by someone sharply intelligent and creative, full of sunshine, rainbows, and wildflowers, on the one hand, and constant touches of melancholy, meaningless, nonetheless – a handsome lie and depressing truth.

The sun would set in front of my eyes as I wait for dusk. It had always been the time when I witnessed nature at its purest. The sun would set in a pool of gold and crimson, spilling the glorious shades all over the dark clouds. The ocean seemed peaceful, almost as if someone had muted the noises of the waves crashing and the birds chirping. For a moment there, I found the peace that I had yearned and ached for such an extended period. At that moment, I did not feel imprisoned or incarcerated. At that moment, I knew that I had the power and ability to conquer the world all alone. I did not feel alone, for I had the glories of nature by my side. And as I would sit there, the dullness, tediousness, disappointments, and unhappiness would wash away with the waves crashing at my feet. At that moment, I did not feel defenseless; I somehow felt complete. At that moment, the propinquity of my heart and the beauties of the world would encounter no boundaries.

But then, as the sun would set and it would be time for me to leave for home, I would get up, and the voices would unmute. I would no longer await the peace for some time, knowing that it seemed beautiful if we were further away from it. The more I longed for it, the more peaceful the peace felt. And I would get up and walk on the sand that desired to swallow my feet. I would leave home with a bucket full of friends, and I would return home empty-handed. But I told myself it was precisely what life is.

The Shark

I lived with my parents and four sisters. Growing up, I thought of my house as a place where we were safe, a place that always treated us right. I presumed it would probably be the only place I would want to come to while life treated me adversely. I did not know how wrong I was. I imagined myself to be thrilled when I became a mature teenager. I thought of my parents as the example that would pop up in the back of my head when I thought about love. Growing up, I always felt like they had a bond that was irreplaceable and rare – a bond that could not be found, no matter how hard one tried to find. Soon I got unveiled to the truth that would remain one of the wickedest memories throughout my life.

All that I had struggled to do was keep going. I had found distractions from the vile taunts of life. The rain had lightened my head, and the ocean had made me feel at peace. At the time, I had not known what life had in store for me. I had not known how fate had planned to kick me down. But with time, the events unfolded in front of my eyes, taking one of the most imperative things in my life away from me. Sometimes, life does not grasp if the victim is a child or an adult, it merely throws hardships, and there is no option left other than holding on or giving up. But at the end of the day, holding on has always been and will always be better than giving up.

In addition to the feelings of being trapped, life had much more devised for me. As I approached my teenage years, my love for the ocean and the rain had augmented. I had made friends from my school, yet the sea and the rain had my trust – for they had been there for me and with me through my worst; they had picked me up whenever I fell, and they had never left my side when the waters got deep and dark. Key West had my love, for it had all that I needed to feel better, everything to cheer me up when I felt like it was all slipping away from my fingers.

Back at home, I had three sisters, including my twin, but I still trusted nature more. I knew that they were my blood, yet I knew that the brilliance and exaltations of the surrounding nature knew precisely what was best for me. We had been close, but not as close as sisters are supposed to be. We talked. We laughed. The house we lived in still felt like home. Although life had been tough lately, my house was a haven for me, at least. Days passed, and we believed we had the perfect family. We trusted that the love my parents had would help us through the toughest of times, even when life turns out to be nothing but a vale of tears. We thought their love would prevail.

But over time, the fights commenced between my parents. We were left terrified because when parents fight, the most affected ones are the children watching them fight. It was not easy for us; it felt like there was no worse turn that life could take. We would shrink in the corner while we viewed the enraged faces of our parents. With those arguments, we started to doubt that there was ever any love between them.

I started to run outside, away from the house, when the disagreements happened. I needed to take a break from all the adversities that life had to offer me. It was not ideal, but I knew that hiding as far away as possible from the house full of confusion would be the most favorable. It made me stronger and more resilient. I got to have some time alone to think things through. I needed to set my life straight because, in the house, I knew I could not. I would easily disappear, and the ocean was my destination every time. It had been a tough time for me, as I got involved with thoughts that were, in no way, healthy for me.

Similarly, one time, my parents had been disagreeing wildly. So, I left the house. I watched the clouds turn dark gray and violent. Minutes later, the clouds thundered vehemently as they crashed into each other, and it started to rain the devil and pitchforks. Though clouds made heavy growling noises, the path was full of tranquility. Maybe I had realized more chaos at home than outside; any amount of noise seemed peaceful to me. Typically, walking in the rain without my shoes on, or the worry of getting wet or sick, I kept going. Because in that rain, I found serenity. It seemed like a type of meditation, an essence of therapy that I did not pay for. Yet, it seemed so beautiful as I wandered among heavy drops, fully present in the moment. It was through the rain that I felt free.

With several more arguments and countless tears, they finalized their divorce. The news hurt us with magnitude much more than even death could ever hurt us. The once happy and content family was now in pieces, and we had no one to turn to. They did not ask us to choose sides. My sisters and I knew that we had to stick together. We knew that the only way to get through this was together. And that was how the journey of our lives started.

It had all been a rough row to hoe. My teenage years had started, and with them, the family was broken into pieces beyond development. My mother and father had moved on in no time, and they had already started new families. My father continued to pay child support for a while and remained close by. The divorce had significant impacts on our personalities, changing us into a whole other person forever.

Following the divorce, I felt like I was unnecessary or just plain lost in the crowd. I felt like I did not matter anymore. I would ask myself, "Did they not think about what would happen if they went through with the divorce?" I kept repeating that inside my head, knowing that the answer was just going to depress me. And so, I would turn to my only true friend – the endless ocean. I knew that no matter what life does to me, no matter how discouraged I fall, no matter how messed up it all gets, the ocean was always going to be there to comfort me. I knew that I was one sunset away from getting fresh. And so, I ran toward the beach as tears flowed from my eyes. Yet I let them fall, not picking up a hand to stop them or scrub them away. I knew they meant I was alive, that I was human.

But only a phase, and exactly like any other, I knew it was transitory and short-lived. I had struggled vigorously to move on from the traumas of my past. Although I had unremittingly felt like I was suffocating, I held on to the hope of a more fantastic future. I tried hard to move on from the sadness that life had sent me. I zealously awaited my eighteenth birthday.

Until the age of 13, I had no childish pleasure in my life. Little girls that age were having birthday parties, shopping for new Christmas dresses, trying to figure out what their next Halloween costumes would be. Not me; I never had any of that, thanks to the restricted religious atmosphere that had consumed my home. I never had a birthday party or even went to one. The Easter Bunny never visited me. I never got to pick out a Halloween costume. I never had a Christmas tree in my house. I knew Santa Claus was unreal, even before I even fully knew who Santa Claus was. I, on the contrary, was not an ordinary girl. I had always been different. The excitement of my eighteenth birthday escalated into grief and apprehensions when I found out my father stopped my child support funds for my mother. He did nothing wrong, as I was now an adult. I think my father was still mad at my mother for choosing a path that broke us apart as a family. To me, it was not about the payment. It was more about feeling further displaced. You see, my father never participated in this religion. But he didn't necessarily know how to protect us from it either. Although I had just turned eighteen, I was still in high school and had my entire future in front of me. I worried about going to college, and I worried about my survival.

Feelings of hurt, confusion, and bewilderment swayed in and paraded over my head, a constant reminder that I was different. The blue feelings would just rush in, telling me that I did not matter as much as I wanted to the people surrounding me. And so, I became quiet. I could not speak much. I could not laugh. I could not smile.

That same day, I went out boating with my high school friends. "God, please make it rain!" I whispered in my heart, hoping the day would turn a bit better. I desperately needed a distraction. I badly needed my pain to subside. The boat took us through the ocean toward an island. The movement terrified everyone, yet I knew I was friends with the ocean. I knew that it would never hurt me. As we approached the island, I hoped it would rain. Along with that, I hoped for many more things in life. And waited for fate to unveil what it had yet to disclose to me.

The sun had reached its zenith and was determined to set soon enough. It shone brilliantly, but the dark clouds prevailed from time to time. The waves had been blessed with distinct shades of gold and blue, and the ocean waves crashed magnificently into each other. As I examined the ocean, I told myself, "Never can there be anything more gorgeous than the ever-evolving ocean." It buzzed with its veiled strength that everyone was familiar with, yet no one could ever utterly comprehend. Home to limitless creatures, the ocean was my home too. As we boated across the waves, we saw little fish diving out of the surface and in. We beheld them yearning for survival in the vast ocean, saving their lives from predator fish. As I understood, I got to thinking life is nothing but a ceaseless struggle to survive in this enormous world, where a few forces endeavor to knock us down.

We reached the island. I had been shadowed and constantly trailed by the feeling of hurt. It had happened earlier that day, and the adverse feelings had bothered me for some time. We put on the snorkeling gear, and I waited no more. I jumped off the boat, and I knew it was how I might feel a bit lighter. I knew that I would feel much restored and ameliorated when

I jumped in the water. And as expected, I felt better. Much better than before. The feelings were still there, but I had buried them deep down. I gave my utter attention and thoughts to the ocean I was in and the waves that splashed against my face. I was not fearful anymore. I did not fear life anymore; I did not fear what it would all turn out to be. At that moment, I was free of all the thoughts holding me back, and finally, I was at peace.

I dove in to further reconnect and explore the beauties of life that the ocean contained. The Coral Reef. The fish swam beautifully, and I liked to think that each of them had a purpose. I liked to believe that they do not just swim around but live out their lives and pass away when they turn old and gray. As I kept my head underwater, I was fascinated by what I saw in front of me.

I once encountered a shark that scanned into my eyes as she swiftly swam toward me. She was not a full-sized shark, but a shark. I stayed in the water, quieter than ever. There was a sort of sudden feeling of fright, panic, and distress, but it did not last. It could not last. "What's the worst it could do?" I asked myself. I stayed in the water, but calmly this time, rather fearlessly. I enjoyed her short company, knowing that the magnificent fish did not mean harm to me; I was entirely in her way. This was her home.

At that moment, I forgot about the hurt for a while. I overlooked the feelings of confusion and bewilderment. For a moment, I did not care about the thoughts that kept telling me that I did not matter as much to the surrounding people. I felt like I was unimportant, but I did not care about any of it at that moment, simply for a brief instant. In this moment, a stranger approached me that did not judge me for everything I had gone through. And so, I remained there, maintaining the art of eye contact as if it were the one thing around which my life revolved. My heartbeat had increased significantly, but not from fear of any kind; it was due to the excitement of being in close proximity to a shark.

She came closer to me while I aimed to sustain eye contact. She came closer to me and opened her mouth a little. She wanted to scare me off, tell me that I did not have anything to fear about or wanted to play; I could never truly fathom. She brushed off against the left side of my body and went away. I turned around and waved her off as she swam away. And at that moment, my heart was at its purest. I felt stronger, like somehow, I had the power to live through life now. I felt like I could face everyone and everything head- on without being knocked down by life. And I was determined to face it all and come out as a winner and survivor.

As I came back to the top of the ocean and took my goggles off, I saw the clouds above me. I took an in-depth breath and sighed, thinking about everything that told me to hold on a little longer. The clouds were dark and gray, and I had hoped for rain all day. The clouds collapsed, and it finally started. The rain started.

That rain was different, much more different from any rain ever before. The other rains had purified my thoughts, but this rain had cleansed my soul. With this rain, I was optimistic about the best of life. With this rain, I was sure everything was going to turn out fine. With this rain, I was captivated to look at everything with a better perception – the glories of nature that make it all so magnificent, the animals that promise you to be there for you through good times and bad, the people that care about you, the agonies that break you, the mistakes that knock you down, the experiences from life that make you, and the hope and expectations that you have from your futures. With this rain, I knew many worthwhile things awaited me in the future. And with this rain, I danced my worries off.

The Return of the Wolf

The Wolves

The feelings of freedom were short-lived. As I returned home, I knew that I was back to everyday life. I knew that I was back to the daily traumas and depressions that life had to offer me. But I knew that hope was significant. So, I gathered all the hope I could during the time I spent in the sea and took it back home. And whenever I felt like I was losing hope, I would simply run toward the ocean faster than a Kentucky Derby horse on the first Saturday in May. I would sit at the shore as the waves gently rub off my feet and move back into the ocean. I would study the setting sun, and that was how I recovered my hope. It was necessary, and I knew I was not the type to give up.

Life went on. The trauma of religion and family had held too much magnitude in my life. But like any other agony and despair, the hurt diminished with the passage of time. My twin sister and I both courageously picked a college in

Boston to start a new life. Together, we learned how to live in the world. I started a job to pay for my living expenses. Without being taught about it, I was on my own. I was independent. Life had still been disheartening for me, yet I kept going. I learned to adapt. I improvised when situations made me feel remorseful. I learned to be gratified.

When college had commenced, the routine was hectic. There was too much workload. Everything was messed up inside my head, and I had no one to take care of me. With my twin sister, I was not alone. But the feelings of solitude and the ghosts of the past would always sway around me at all times. I made friends, but none of them felt like home. I met people, yet I did not hold them close to me. I was afraid of the hurt. The past had been stained much, so I dissociated myself from any potential trauma and melancholy.

It all turned into sunshine and wildflowers for a while when I met a boy while I was in college. We became friends, and he was the first friend that felt like a friend. He assured me that he was going to be there for me when the flowers withered, and the waters got deep. He had his ambitions and goals in life – he wanted to be an actor in Hollywood. But somehow, it all felt real. Somehow, I was unable to catch up or comprehend that it was nothing but a play that I was part of. I had sustained to keep the walls around me up and intact, and no one could ever get past them. But this person did. He forced me to pull my walls down while I believed I had fallen. But the thing about love is that the person who hurts you is the same person whom you want to confront and comfort yourself.

As we progressed from friends to more than just friends, I had expected things from him. I was captivated to believe that he was the one I would spend my nights dreaming about, the one who would hold me when I cried, the one who would laugh with me, the one whom I would love endlessly and without any limits. I wanted to believe that I did, with all my heart, and for some time in my life, I did.

He made me feel like I was the sunshine of the eternal dawn within; he made me feel like I was the one who made it safe for his soul to breathe anew. He made me feel like I was the most essential part of his life. He made me feel like I was the courage he imagined was long extinguished from his world. He had told me that the reason he felt this way for me was who I was, that my touch was energy, and all that I was to him was home.

The first time we kissed was magical. He had maintained eye contact with me as if my fragile and sylphlike features were the most imperative things to him. He pulled my head slowly toward him as we both closed our eyes and left it on fate to play its part. In that kiss, there was the mellifluousness of passion, combined with care and deep affection. A million thoughts rushed into my head as our lips collided, but the thought that prevailed over all others was that the person I was kissing was essential to me. In that kiss, I was genuinely pure and highly vulnerable, and it gave me enough strength to fight the world if he was by my side. The kiss flowed through my body and blossomed underneath the facade of my skin. For a few moments, I had forgotten about my past, and I had forgotten how I had missed my home because, in that kiss, I was home.

College life went on. Toward the end of college, I had been given a thesis assignment to prepare for. I thought a lot about it. I had much to write about; my life was, after all, was a story to write about. The topic was shortlisted to be about the 1995 reintroduction of wolves back into Yellowstone National Park. Wolves had been extirpated from Yellowstone National Park in the 20th century. They were reintroduced back into Yellowstone National Park in 1995. While writing, I understood the wolves. I knew that I was growing fond of the lifestyle of the wolves. After all, they are intelligent, caring, and playful animals who care deeply about their families. They stick together in packs and fight together. They educate the baby wolves, and they help the injured. They are loyal to the pack, never thinking about turning their backs on one another.

While writing, I developed a profound fondness for this animal. I had developed the desire to see a wolf pack in the wild once in my lifetime. I knew deep down in my heart that I had formed a protective bond for the wolves. Wolves are the most victimized and mistreated animals in the world. The world thinks of wolves only as predators. People think they are dangerous in some way. I was so drawn into the negative connotations people had about bringing these predators back to Yellowstone National Park. But if you ask me, no big bad wolf is lurking around out there in the shadows somewhere. I loathe the story of "little red riding hood" and "the three little pigs." They are not there to tear you into little pieces. What a farce these stories are, which easily poison the minds of children about wolves. During the writing process of that thesis, all I could think about was going out to the West and encountering a wolf in the wild – how magnificent it would look. All I wanted was to go out into the wild and see for myself why the wolves were considered so grave and threatening. One day, one way or another, I would go. My thesis was complete.

Finally, came along my graduation day, the day I had anxiously awaited for many years. Almost every student had their parents there for the ceremony, and it reminded me of what I had missed out on. Alternatively, it also reminded me of what I had been through in life and how I had gotten over all of it. I remember feeling completely out of gas after college. Constantly reminded me of what I had missed out on. Whereas it also reminded me of what I had been through in life and how I had gotten over all of it. So instead of attending my graduation ceremony, I chose to drive. All I wanted was to drive far, far away. Drive into a new journey. Although my path took me to the Pacific Ocean, the wholehearted thought of heading to wolf country did cross my mind.

My relationship with that Boston boy was not long-lived. It ended shortly after my graduation. He was my first everything. I had loved him, but the one-sidedness of the relationship was getting toxic for me. I never could know if it affected him the way it affected me. I often wondered if he was ever thinking about me the same way I was thinking about him. But at the end of the day, this voice that tells me, "You don't need anyone. All you need is yourself. Get yourself together and face it all. You are going to turn out fine. It is all going to be splendid." That voice is what my heart and soul would say nightly that I would spend overthinking everything about my life.

Like anything else in this world, the love was not forever. Things could not work out for many reasons, and I was left behind. Knowing that I was just another "girl" in his journey to the top of Hollywood was an eye-opener. I was once again left behind. But this time, I was prepared. I was prepared for yet another heartbreak. Because the previous heartbreaks had taught me how to get over one when it happens another time in life. Even though it broke me to the core, I knew how to control my feelings. I felt apathy from the inside, but my brain did not tell me to give up, and neither did my heart. I knew I could get through it. So, I pictured this Boston boy as one of the little tadpoles I had raised. It was now his turn to go off into the wild. And just like that, I accepted his departure.

With time, the hurt tapered to the point where it did not matter anymore. Sure, I thought about it. It's burdensome watching his face pop up on the big screen from time to time. But what mattered was it added to my experience. Keeping aside the hurt and the time it took to get over it all, I was doing fine living with my twin sister. I did not have a best friend, but I did have my twin sister's shoulder to cry on, yet I knew that all I needed was myself. Because in the end, we are all that we need. In the end, we are the only ones that we could trust.

On the day of my graduation, I was pleased and sad. I missed my parents. I wanted them to be there and stand up and clap for me when they called out my name. I wanted them to be proud of me for all the hard work I had done and all the things that life had thrown my way. I picked myself up after every fall, even when there was no one there to pick me up. All the setbacks, yet I had my head tall. I wanted them to be proud of me for the first time.

But at the end of the day, that is exactly what life is. We do not always get what we want. Maybe it is because it is life's way of telling us it has better things planned for us ahead. Maybe it is life telling us that the thing we want is not reasonably fitting for us. Anyway, it is life, and we do not always get what we want. As I stood there, my degree in hand, my eyes became watery. And I asked God, "Now what?". I looked at the sky and whispered, "why me?" A part of me replied, "because you can bear it. Most people can't." The clouds had already turned dark and gray. And as always,

I had longed for the rain. As I looked up to the skies, attempting to talk to God or whomever the higher authority was, the clouds crashed into each other. It started to rain, and I awaited it to cleanse my heart, mind, and soul all over again.

Losing Rain

When I was in college, I remember studying some surprising facts about the brain. Did you know that our brain has this inbuilt mechanism for suppressing painful memories? The brain can make you "forget" that something painful happened to you because. According to the brain, it counts as a traumatizing event. It is believed this is a coping mechanism for the brain to protect itself from remembering something too stressful.

But if that is the case, why can I recall this memory as clear as day? Why is this day stored in my brain crystal clear? The day felt like everything I was and everything I wanted to do was crushed by the weight of the world? The day I questioned my existence. The day I wanted to give up. The day I lost everything.

I remember sitting opposite my OB/GYN, right after I had had a routine ultrasound. She had a still expression on her face; it was hard to read. But I knew something unpleasant was coming up. It was only a hunch, and hunches are never wrong, are they?

Sometimes you make choices in your life and learn from those choices. During my dating years, I felt like I was in a pond of tadpoles searching for the right frog to kiss and become my Prince.

I had not dated much, but the frogs I have dated were so different in so many ways. I was looking in all the wrong places. The only thing these frogs had in common was being more broken than me. Was I searching to fix them because the thing I wanted to fix was "me"?

Under my daily showers, I would dream of marrying a real Prince from the Royal Monarchy. I always had a thing for Prince Harry. But I wanted my own King to give me all the crown jewels in life. Through this fantasy, I became knowledgeable in the Royal Family, and my loyal affection for Queen Elizabeth II remains until this day.

In the end, I did not have to look far to find my King. He was here in Key West all along. A handsome, intelligent Midwestern boy from America's hometown of Hannibal, Missouri. He has gifted me with true happiness, children, and even tiny diamond and stone replicas of all the crown jewels of England purchased from Windsor Castle in London. Being a twin, I always wanted to have twins. Together, we had twin boys. A third baby boy followed. Two years later, I was pregnant with a little girl. There was no doubt in my mind she would be called "Rain". After having three boys, I longed for this little girl. What a beautiful flower she would be to add to my already perfect garden.

My husband and I did not "plan" to have another baby. It had just happened. And I didn't realize I was pregnant until morning sickness took its course. I was in the restroom throwing up when somewhere in between it hit me. I began calculating the last time I got my period, and it was already six weeks late.

I remember being so happy, my emotions finding no limits. My eyes had started to water at the thought that I would soon be a mother again. There was nothing more soothing than knowing that I would be giving life to another small baby.

I had always been someone drawn to children. I loved being around them, playing with them, and talking to them. But when they would cry, in those moments, I would cover my ears and wait until it was over. But when I stood there in the shower, I realized how love was natural and how it crept into my heart out of nowhere, making me ready to even put my life on the line for this baby.

As a twin myself, I had always secretly wished for twins. Followed by another third son. My life felt at the peak of happiness and fulfillment. Then I became pregnant with this little girl. Even though we were not planning this pregnancy, I was just as excited as if it were my first time

Our visit to the doctor was perfect. The feeling was raw and unfiltered. I felt like I was happy, but I also felt nervous. When I laid down on the bed and let the doctor put the gel on my belly, it felt queasy. My husband had reached out for my hand then, and I could feel my heart beating at the speed of ten thousand racehorses.

As soon as we heard the heart beating on the monitor, everything felt calm. My mind, my heart. Every part of my body felt calm. Like suddenly, everything had started to make sense. As if everything felt newer and better. That night, I had the soundest most sleep that I'd had in years. I had hummed the tune "somewhere over the rainbow" to my unborn baby, to soothe it and myself. And I had slipped into oblivion just like that.

I remember making the next trip to the doctor when I was twelve weeks pregnant, and then fourteen. My belly had started growing a little, and I was still nauseous in the morning. There were things I enjoyed eating and foods I would throw up at the sight of.

My second visit to the doctor was perfectly normal, and so was the third. However, it was then that I found out that we were expecting a baby girl. Every time I returned from the doctor, I would feel excited, unable to hold back my emotions, and simply waiting for the baby to come out already. I didn't know it was possible to fall in love so intensely with someone you haven't even seen or met properly. After I knew that a girl was taking form in my belly, I wanted to name her with the only other thing I loved as much as I loved her… Rain.

I was so lost in the happiness of it that I forgot nothing attracts a serpent quite like it. That's the thing about love; it has the permanence of a rainbow... Beautiful while it's there, and just as likely to have disappeared by the time you blink.

And I had blinked.

And my longing for perfection was being destroyed.

I was almost 20 weeks along in my pregnancy when my OB/GYN gave me that expression for at least five minutes before she finally broke the ice.

"Gloria..." she had opened her mouth to say. I watched her with a keen expression on my face. My husband would usually tag along in every appointment, but this time he was caught up in some work. I didn't mind it at all since I expected everything to be normal. But when talking about life... Can you expect anything that's too normal?

While strings and strings of words were escaping the mouth of the doctor, I could feel nothing but heavy. A consistent "ting" was ringing in my ears, and I wanted to run. From the doctor's view. From the world. From myself.

The only words I can recall from that speech are "complications" and "surgery," "soon," and "do you understand?"

I nodded my head and went back home, mentally preparing myself for the event that I would be taking a course very soon. I told my husband what had come out of the visit I had paid to the doctor that day. He said nothing, only hugged me and kissed my forehead, trying to be the strong one.

I hadn't cried yet. Partially because I felt nothing; all I could feel was numb. My head was clouded, and my heart was still. I didn't cry, also because I was in denial. And that is rarely a good thing.

So that is how I was set to lose my unborn daughter, who was to be named Rain, in the fall of 2014. My 20-week pregnancy was ending right before my eyes due to unforeseen complications. After several invasive prenatal tests, my doctor informed me my child was dying inside of me due to an unfortunate genetic disorder called Trisomy 18. Within a week of this earth-shattering news, I was on an operating table, knowing I would never look at or hold my daughter. The heartache was unbearable. I did not want to wake up from what was about to happen.

The denial had worked for the days that I had spent before the surgery, but as soon as I entered the hospital, I felt like I had entered a state of emotional turmoil. And the toll it had taken on me was more than just simple grief... It was the type of sadness that weighs you down. The kind that makes you want to disappear, like wanting the Earth to swallow you whole.

I felt my heart struggling for strength. I could feel it getting heavier with every passing second. I could feel myself entering the black hole of despair and falling down deep in the pit.

It seemed like they were not cutting into my stomach, but my heart. I knew that the pain of cutting into my stomach was nothing compared to the pain left from the hole that would form by the time I got through this. And that's why I dreaded the thought of waking back up with all the heartache before the surgery that I would have to endure. Deep in my heart, I am ashamed to admit that a part of me did not want to wake up. And if I didn't know any better, I would say it was justified. My heart, body, and soul were broken beyond repair.

Or at least that's what I thought. Because what happened during surgery was exceptional... something that changed my life forever. That's the funny thing about fate... It sneaks up on you when you least expect it.

During the surgery, I felt the moment my daughter left my body. And I was gifted a vivid and unearthly dream. In my dream, a wolf pack surrounded me.

The wolves were beautiful, now that I can recall them clearly in my head. Grays, blacks, and whites, with hypnotizing, yellow eyes. The wolves were coming close to my face, one by one as if trying to say something. They just stood there, close to my face, staring at me. One rather large gray and tan wolf stayed the longest by my side. She was comforting me in a motherly way.

It took me a while to understand that they were trying to communicate by nudging me. But I did not move... All because I did not want to. The pain running through my veins was so painful. But that is exactly what the wolves were there to stop me from. I didn't know that until later after my surgery, sometime after when I had the time and sense to understand.

Remember what I told you about the brain? That it is surprising? Well, how the wolves communicated with my subconscious and said it all... saved my life.

Little by little, and one by one… the wolves made their way towards my lifeless body resting on the cold, unsympathetic table. Even though I couldn't move, I could still hear them, see them, and feel them.

Their presence had a calming impact on my dream. I could feel them gathered around me, telling me it was too soon to give up. They did not have to say it out loud. Being in their presence, looking into their eyes, I understood what they were trying to tell me.

I looked at them, one by one, each having something different to say and yet delivering the same message to me.

"Don't give up."

"Be strong."

"You have much to look forward to."

"There is more to life than just sadness."

"We can go through this together."

"Follow us."

Anyone knowing that I was "connected" with wolves would feel weird, but that was the only thing that kept me going. The only thing that brought a glimmer of hope in the dark tunnel where I was locked and lost in.

Connecting with the pack of wolves brought me calmness, and I felt like my soul was finally at peace. How did these wolves enter my subconscious mind...? I have no idea. But they did save me... from the darkness, the pain, the hurt... and most of all... from myself. If it wasn't for them, I don't think I would have the power to wake up after my surgery and continue.

I presume we rely too much on other people for our happiness, support, and peace. There are other things, other beings who contribute, if not more, than exactly as much. And I realized that after I woke up from my dream.

Here, I thought my life had reached its limit because I lost my daughter. I thought I would never get past that agonizing pain and forget the unfortunate event that had seeped through my life. But scars fade, and wounds heal.

The appearance of the wolves in my dream had to mean something... there had to be a reason for it. These wolves didn't only give me hope; they regenerated me. And most importantly, these wolves told me sometimes... Some blessings we get in life also come by shattering all windows.

Alone in Yellowstone

Unlike most of the things in life, the dream I had during surgery did not escape my thoughts solely like that. It lingered, piercing its way through my head, consuming me entirely. But in a virtuous way, as I always think of the "how's" and "why's" of these wolves and their existence in my life.

I always feel like I am at a loss for words when I try to explain this experience. The emotional rush, the surge of hope, and the connection that I felt were so strong; it almost felt unreal.

Most people will have a hard time believing that this is true. Most people who will read this will find this experience surreal, untrue, that something like this is only a dream, a ridiculous idea that stems from fantasy or fiction. But then there is the other half of the population that exists in this wild world, the people who believe memories are more than just thoughts that roam around and persist in our heads. Sometimes, they are messages, the connection from the people or the beings who we foresee in our heads. They call out to us and sometimes even intrude, and make their presence known in unconscious ways. They are hints for us that tell us that we must reconnect, whether it's a person, a force of nature, a place, or all of them. Something that gives us a sense of belonging, something that tells us that we are not alone in this world. That's all we need to hear. That's all anyone needs to hear. Life is tough on its own and knowing that there is something that you can relate to or share the same experience, makes it slightly tolerable.

Losing a child, losing anyone, is not the type of pain one can go through alone. You do need someone who can understand what you went through, how you felt, and how you feel in the aftermath of the event.

When I knew I had to let go of my daughter for a split second, I felt like the Earth had stopped spinning. My world had collapsed entirely in front of my eyes, and for every moment that I had felt that I should go on, this felt like it had all gone in vain. I wanted everything to slow down.

But what I didn't know was what was coming my way. I didn't know that during my surgery, something so unbelievable would happen, I would feel anew.

I don't know how it happened. But I do know that from that day on, after waking up from my dreadful experience, I felt a new inner strength inside of me. This energy coursing through my veins, and I felt like something deep inside of me had changed. The wolves drew me in with the words they said. The aspects of the dream fascinated me. It felt strangely comforting. As if this was the one thing I had been waiting for my entire life.

I didn't know how to deal with it at first. I didn't know what I should do with the dream; I didn't know what to think or feel. The experience, at first, was immense considering how I felt the wolves had come to me with a purpose.

I expected that as time passed, the memory of this dream would get faint and fainter until one day, it would be eradicated. But it was too strong, and with each passing day, I was drawn more and more to those wolves in my dream. Especially their message that said, "Follow us."

It took me a while to reach a conclusion for the dream. But after a few months, I felt ready. I was ready to explore this attraction.

I set foot towards this journey, *my* journey, a calling from the wolves. Eventually, I followed that calling to Yellowstone National Park; I don't know why. It seemed like the right thing to do. I decided to stay in Cooke City, Montana, as it was one of the closest towns into Lamar Valley, the valley of the wolves. I had become familiar with Cooke City through the writings of Ernest Hemingway while growing up in the Florida Keys.

I didn't feel nervous, even once. All I could think of was the answer I needed for the why's and the how's. It was a strange adventure, but it brought me comfort, knowing that I was possibly one step closer to meeting the truth.

On this specific morning, I was driving into Yellowstone through the Northeast entrance when I noticed this beautiful open round prairie. The sight was entrancingly lovely, and I was wonderstruck. Suddenly, I felt like the prairie was begging me to stop. There was a sudden surge in my heart telling me to take a while and just be there.

At that moment, I felt the need to touch the Earth... feel the grasses, smell the flowers, breathe the air, and altogether lose myself in there. The compulsion was so strong that I couldn't stop myself. So, I parked my car and walked out.

I kept treading in the prairie until I was far out. When I reached the middle, I decided to sit down. I nestled myself in between the sage and willows. It was peaceful. I just sat there surrounded by all this beautiful wilderness landscape. For a split-second, it was all perfect. Everything felt alright, like there was no space for evil in the world. For that moment, I felt like I had finally reached where I was supposed to be.

And then that moment ended.

Suddenly, I felt a rush of emotions flood my brain. Everything felt so raw, the anger, the angst, the hurt, the pain... everything felt like it had reached a new intensity, a level too much for me to handle. I could feel hot tears forming in my eyes. It was devastating; it was too much. I couldn't take anything else in; I couldn't help myself.

So, I curled up into a ball and began weeping. I wept and wept until my tears began running dry.

But I was not alone in this pain, anger, and hurt. I had never been alone. The Earth had begun weeping with me, every raindrop falling on the dry ground synchronizing with the teardrop that rolled down my cheek and towards my neck.

The memory of those fresh raindrops remains unfaded in my head. Raindrop by raindrop, cleansing the Earth as the tears cleansed my soul.

Like I said, I was not alone. Within a few moments, I could feel a strong presence nearby. I prayed for my heart to be still and started looking here and there. But I didn't have to search at all, because the moment I looked up, she was there.

Sitting directly in front of me was a lone black wolf. She has settled some 50 yards away… And she was looking at me. Like really *looking*. I knew she could see through me, and instantly, I was reminded of my dream. The wolf was looking through my soul. And all I could feel was at peace. As if suddenly, every emotion I felt was sidelined.

71

Everything was pushed towards the back of my head, and the only thing that prevailed was peace.

Suddenly, a thought crossed my mind. Was I dreaming? Maybe. Maybe not.

I was unsure, but it all felt so familiar.

I glanced up at the wolf, and she glanced at me too. We stared at each other for a while before we locked our eyes, and we kept staring. When I blinked, she blinked back. I knew that we were connected; I could feel it.

I could feel the strength in her eyes. Like her, I too could perceive her soul. I could feel her entirely, her soul, her purpose. I realized that she was there to help me heal from the pain that I was feeling. I knew she was here to help me evolve. Just like how the wolves had appeared in my dream.

I could feel her communicating to me, and I was listening. She was there... and so was I. We could feel each other, and there was nothing that made me feel better than the thought that she and I could finally understand each other… face-to-face. I shared both time and space with this wild black wolf. She and I were the only ones there. We were alone. The connection we had was extraordinary… It was telepathic, magical, and almost untrue.

The surge of emotions that I had begun feeling was all I needed to hold onto. I needed more of it. I wanted more… I decided not to move. I decided I would not leave. This wolf would have to depart first on this day because I would not.

Somehow, I managed enough strength to lift my iPhone to try and snap one quick photo of this encounter. I needed proof to believe this was happening.

Snap.

I took the photo. And she let me. The photo is worth more than gold to me. That's the thing I like about photographs. They are proof that once, even if only for a heartbeat, everything was perfect.

And at that moment, everything was indeed perfect. During this hour of alone time with this wolf, I learned so much about myself. Humans often lack confidence and belief. And for me, the case was not any different.

Yes, we are indeed surrounded and supported by the people close to us. But most of us don't believe the words they utter to us to make us feel better. We can't feel better unless we go through a certain situation and understand what we have learned, lost, and gained from it.

"You don't know how strong you are until you have no choice but to be strong."

I don't know how many times I have heard this statement in my life. What I know is I did not understand it until I felt the loss of my child. That moment changed my life forever.

We all come into this world alone, and we die alone. Every situation that we pass is alone. But that doesn't mean we have to be lonely. And with the right people or beings, you can never be lonely.

And that's just one thing that I learned from my encounter with this wolf on that day. That even though you might have to go through troubles alone, there will always be someone to help you get through the emotional toll you will be taking. Be it happy or unhappy; there might always be someone on the lookout for you.

In that one hour I spent with this wolf, I also felt a type of healing. All my life, I had felt like something had been missing. And that came from the wolf, a gift she gave me on that day. She encouraged me to find the strength and courage to place myself in the context of the world as it is. She taught me that I was never alone, and every time I felt low, I could always look up to her for help.

When it was time for her to rejoin her pack, she briefly stopped and looked back at me. I wasn't ready to let go of her; I had yet to thank her for all the things that she had given me so effortlessly.

When she stared at me, I silently thanked her. She blinked. I blinked back. It was a message, and I understood. I knew I would see her again.

Later that evening, I found out this black wolf was 926F, the alpha female of the Lamar Canyon Pack. "926F" refers to her being the 926th female wolf collared by The Wolf Project in Yellowstone National Park. She was all I needed to hold on to, hopefully, just a little bit more. She was the daughter of the original infamous she-wolf 832F, aka "06" and 755M. Both her parents were former alphas of the Lamar Canyon Pack. Both lost to her by the time we met.

And that's when I knew that she too had known what true loss was. That is also when I remembered the face from my dream... It was her mother. And I knew that we could feel each other's pain.

But that was only the beginning of it. I decided it was time for me to start visiting, a friend, a mentor, a motivator... A soulmate. I decided to keep coming back for her as long as possible, and as much as possible. I wanted her to know that I understood and that she too wasn't alone. I wanted to share more time and space with this wild black wolf alone. It was an extraordinary telepathic soul connection that is now and forever in my "blood memory."

Returning and Learning

In the years that followed, every time I visited the park, I searched for her and her pack. There was no time I went to Yellowstone and did not spot her. Sometimes it was before the sun came up. Other times it was when the moon was out. Each time, the experience would be new and fulfilling. Each time I learned something, something, each time I let go of my grief a little more.

I didn't believe that it was possible. But it was happening. Because I had a wild wolf who was living life exactly like mine. From feeling the loss to coping with it, there is nothing I will give credit for to anyone else, except her, Wolf 926F.

Grief is like a lengthy, bottomless pit, a pit where there is nothing but darkness, where you are alone, and you know there is no way out. No one can hear you; no one knows where you are. Grief is heavy; it consumes you entirely. But only if you let it.

And until I met Wolf 926F, I was letting grief take its course. And then something changed, and Wolf 926F came to me like a blessing. She was the light that lit up my tunnel, and I realized there was much more that I had to learn, much more that I had to investigate, discover, and fall in love with.

On most days, I felt like a hunter. Scanning. Searching. Watching. Listening. Even before I noticed her, I felt her. For the next few years, I witnessed this wolf gain everything, only to lose it, over and over again. But never once had I ever seen her give up on life completely. And that was something that would always bring me strength. She would always remain in charge of herself, her pups, and her pack. She knew she had to be there for everyone.

I have many treasured stolen moments with Wolf 926F. She is the main reason why I keep coming back to Yellowstone. Truth be told, she still is. She had become my teacher. And I learned more than merely a few things from her.

Bravery, strength, courage, trust, confidence, belief... She was more than just ordinary.

She would always find the courage to do everything that would seem impossible. I frequently catch myself thinking, "What would Wolf 926F do?" She had the mindset of a queen. The heart of a warrior. The instincts of a survivor. The ideas of a leader. She was everything all at once.

You understand, by the time we locked eyes during our first encounter, Wolf 926F had already been through every hardship I had been through. Losing a parent. Losing a mate. Losing a sibling. Losing a child. Yet, she always remained in control. And she did not let anything affect her. She was mourning, I knew she was, but her attitude towards life never changed. She was smarter than any human I have ever met.

Throughout the years, it became evident that Wolf 926F and I lived parallel lives. The solidification of this is strongly based on the last time I saw her during the Fall of October

2018. She, along with her mate "Small Dot" and daughter "Little T", was gallantly showing off their five new pups for the first time after an elusive summer. From far away, I could see her proudly showing off two of those pups, which some say were "her twins." Yet again, another parallel moment. A mixture of serendipity and personal experience was shared, as I also recently gave birth to twins.

No matter how many times I do this, time slows down when I arrive in the Greater Yellowstone ecosystem, consisting of Yellowstone National Park and the Grand Tetons. Sometimes it's a perfect morning. But in a few hours, that will change rapidly. Temperatures fall and rise without notice. I come prepared. I love this new place I now affectionately call my home-away-from-home. What I observe out in the wild within the lives of these wolves surpasses experiences in my own life. I admire these wolves. I have the honor of observing them in their wild on my own terms. My heart runs with them when I see them running freely as a pack. My heart aches with them at the constant loss of pack members, be it by mother nature or human hatred. Grief is a form of love. This Love hurts. This type of Love holds hands tightly with grief. I grieve for this species that fights to hang on. But for someone who loves these wolves, I want so much more for them than just survival.

I remember this one early Spring Day, specifically when I was looking for Wolf 926F. I remember this day from something that happened to me. Something that caught me off guard.

While I was looking for her, I was bluff charged by a huge grizzly bear. I was standing peacefully, minding my business, doing nothing except searching for my friend. When and how the grizzly bear noticed me, I am still unable to recall.

The grizzly bear was probably fresh out of hibernation. He directly bluff charged at me within 10 feet. I remember feeling unusually calm as if I had already been prepared for this situation. Although, I give this credit to Wolf 926F.

I learned from watching her to slowly stand my ground and remain still. Make no eye contact with the grizzly bear. A scream or sudden movement might trigger an attack. I did have my can of bear spray, but never felt threatened enough to use it. Even when it stood on its hind legs to get a better view, I knew that a standing bear is a curious bear, not a threatening one. Bears usually do not want to attack you; they want to be left alone. I may have imagined a glimpse of my life flash in front of me that morning. But I found comfort knowing that nothing would go wrong, since the grizzly bear and I had crossed paths for a reason.

I should have felt more scared than I did. But it was unbelievable. I also felt strength in knowing that both this grizzly bear and I were both here for a reason. For a short moment, our paths crossed, and we both left in peace and went about our business. He departed through his escape route, and I through mine. Respectfully, this was his home, and I was the uninvited guest. At that moment, sharing time and space, I was not afraid. Not even for a second did it cross my mind that I was in some sort of danger.

I could feel my heart being captured by the beauty of the wild, yet again. So, close I could smell him. So close I could see the blood smeared all over his face from his fresh breakfast. For everyone, the situation might have been horrifying, but to me, it seemed like a connection. There was so much belief in my heart that there must be a specific reason why this grizzly bear and my path collided. I felt lost in the beauty of the universe and its timing again.

There is nothing I would want to change about the encounter. And if I had chosen between a different scenario that could have happened, I would still choose this crossing. Maybe I have no reason for it... But it feels right. And when your gut tells you that something is right, there is generally no room left for doubt to grow there.

And after the grizzly bear incident, it became clearer to me that there was more than just one reason why our paths crossed on this day. My respect and admiration for grizzly bears is now bigger than me.

Wolf 926F was not only my parallel companion, but she has also been passing on several values and attributes to me. I had learned so many noble virtues from her. And with every encounter, I felt like my life was taking a turn, and for the better. I felt like I was turning into a better person myself.

But when I met the grizzly bear, what I learned from him was different from what I picked from Wolf 926F. He taught me faith… in the universe and its timing. There are so many things we believe are coincidental when they are actually "put" timely for you to experience. Even if the event is initially negative, there will always be a positive side that will show itself in the long run. It can be anything, patience, tolerance, self-care, diligence, kindness, faith, hope… And so much more.

My experience with nature has always brought me peace. Even if the situation was a bitter pill to swallow sometimes, there is always a way to get out of it. That too takes shape or form from nature itself.

I lost my child at the hands of whatever higher power there is in nature and within nature. I found my comfort. It almost felt like the perfect give and take situation. Of course, my heart still weeps for Rain, but simultaneously, I have found comfort knowing that there is someone who felt the same pain. And with that, she helped me get out of it before I could fall deep, deep down in the bottomless pit of grief.

Wolf 926F helped me learn the most calming and successful way of escaping danger. But the grizzly bear taught me something important. That there is no such thing as "always contented" or "always calm." Sometimes, your energies are so exhausted they leave you for a while; they give you the space to breathe. During this time, you do many things because you feel like you have lost control over everything you do. You scream, you yell, and you get frustrated. And once the energies feel like you have had enough space, they return to you, making you stronger and better than you were before. More capable of handling a situation. More capable of understanding things clearly. And more capable of letting your best self-work in a situation.

So, even though the experience with this grizzly could have easily been unpleasant, I learned the importance of self-belief. My love and loyalty to grizzly bears are partly due to this encounter, but mostly attributed to Grand Teton Grizzly Bear 399. She is yet another wild creature that has taught me, through years of observations, about the challenges and sacrifices of being a mother. Just recently, she slowly paraded her four yearling cubs within ten yards of my parked car. As always, she was cool, calm, and collected. She knows her path. Humans have played a part in the success of how this grizzly bear successfully raises her cubs. Although a little too close for comfort, our eyes have locked. I watch her; she watches me. I blink. She blinks back. This is a familiar feeling. I am a mother. She is a mother. She is 25 now. She is a legend. A gift of the wild. Nothing compares. I hold my breath respectfully as she passes by within 5 feet of my face. She keeps one eye on me as each cub takes their turn in passing by. This is her home. I am the intruder. All hail to the Queen of the Tetons. Forever the Matriarch of these Mountains.

Besides, I also learned how much I loved returning to the Greater Yellowstone Ecosystem, and how much I loved being around the wolves and grizzly bears. It has been a routine practice for me, and never once would I miss a chance to be with them, see them and learn new things from them.

Coming to visit with Wolf 926F would always feel like coming up for fresh air. Being around her always seemed like she saved me from drowning. She was a small creature, but her influence on my life was monumental. I went from the depths of despair to wishing for one more day to see her. And everything I learned… I learned from her.

Her existence in my life isn't entirely about the "things" I learned from her. It was always soothing to watch her sit down, walk around the valley, look after her pack, and howl. And the virtues she passed down to me are an additional bonus. Because if it weren't for these bonuses, I might not have been able to thrive.

I'm singing in the rain

Just singing in the rain

What a glorious feelin'

I'm happy again

I'm laughing at clouds

So dark up above

The sun's in my heart

And I'm ready for love

Let the stormy clouds chase

Everyone from the place

Come on with the rain

I've a smile on my face

I walk down the lane

With a happy refrain

Just singin',

Singin' in the rain

Dancin' in the rain.

Farewell Wolf 926

The last time I saw Wolf 926F was in the fall of 2018. I can never forget that day; it was one of my most treasured memories in the wild.

Wolf 926F finally came out of hiding to show the world her grace and strength after an elusive summer. She walked tall, gratified that she showed the world that had given her so much pain she had again become a mother. A mother of twins, maybe more. The happiness in her eyes was shining, making her eyes look like citrine crystals. I was as happy for her as she was herself to become a mother again. I felt like somehow, I was part of her family. But like we often forget, happiness is short-lived, and in the blink of a moment, we all lose it at the hands of fate. Wolf 926F was the most important wild animal I have ever encountered. Through her, I learned how to navigate life's hardships. She was, she is, and she will always be part of my life. Her hardships were my hardships. Her happiness was my happiness. When she got hurt, I would hurt. When she lost, I lost. When she won, I won. When she was strong, I was strong. When she grieved, I grieved. When she lost a parent, I lost a parent. When she lost a pup, I lost a child. And when she was taken from this earth, a piece of me was taken along with her.

In the manner of how she was taken, that instantly will always be a trigger of anger and sadness within me. But as I have learned from watching her survive against all odds in the wild, a broken heart still beats. To be honest, I don't want to figure that out. I don't want to know why someone would do such a cruel thing.

I remember it vividly, her trotting behind her pups as she urged them to move further. It was an early evening in the fall of October 2018. She came out and sat proudly behind her twin pups... Her pups will now continue her legacy in the valley of the wolves. But she would never get the chance to raise them. And nothing breaks my heart more, knowing that she will never play a role in her pup's life. Maybe she is watching over them from a distance... At least, I like to think so.

Late November 2018, one month after I saw her, Wolf 926F was shot and killed by a hunter from Cooke City. She was killed just a few miles outside the park in Silvergate, Montana, near the northeast entrance to Yellowstone.

I never got to see her for the last time. Maybe because I left thinking I would come soon, but it was too late. And that's the thing... You never actually know that the last time is the last ... You think you have forever, but you don't.

Some say she was targeted for who and what she was. An alpha wolf. And that was possibly the worst reason anyone could have come up with. How can someone be so merciless, killing animals who don't even harm them? All Wolf 926F wanted at this time in her life was to be a mother. Through observations, it appeared she had recently relinquished her alpha status to her daughter, who was next in line for the throne, and everything was taken away from her so harshly. She was stripped of everything, and her pups were left motherless.

When I heard the news, my heart shattered into a million pieces. I felt like once again, everything in my world was spinning, and it would all collapse on top of me. My heart was beating too fast for words to explain, and I did not have the strength to build myself up again. I needed a strong answer to why something like this would happen, but nothing made sense anymore.

I sat down, thinking of every reason why someone would want to kill this wolf. A series of questions revolved around my head; how will I gather strength inside of me to accept what has happened? How will I deal with the anger trapped inside of my body? Will I ever forget what happened? Will I ever reason?

Rain. I need to be in the rain. Rain has always saved me from pain. I ran upstairs in my quiet shower, and I cried for almost two hours under the running water, closing my eyes pretending it was wild rain.

Why her? Why now? What would Wolf 926F do? I know what she would do. Take. Learn. Let go. Accept. Move Forward.

It's natural. You must live as you breathe. Taking and releasing. It is the cycle of life. We should accept it and integrate it into our daily lives. But I am not a wolf. However, what she taught me was invaluable. The foundation of survival instinct exists within us prior to learned experience.

But when you are dealing with a loss, you lose your sense of self. No matter how hard you try, you cannot function properly because the entire situation is too overwhelming for you to handle. You feel a series of emotions, from shock or anger to disbelief, guilt, and profound sadness. You don't think straight; you have a hard time eating, sleeping, and even, performing the simplest of tasks. And that's not even the worst part.

The worst part is you question yourself, question your entire existence, and question why you are stuck in an endless loop of sadness and why you can't seem to get out of it. But I learned that there is nothing wrong with it. I understood that we are humans, and our own emotions defeat us.

Regardless of what the intensity of a situation is or what the loss is, a person will always feel a greater toll on their emotional stance compared to their physical health.

And for me, it wasn't any different. The death of Wolf 926F deeply affected me. I have always been an emotional person, but I did have a grip on them. I would only allow them to flow when I felt like there was a need to. Especially after my daughter was taken away from me, I learned to become better at handling my emotions. I became significantly stable when it came to managing them. For all of which, I will give the credit to Wolf 926F.

Wolf 926F was more than just some wild animal to me. She had taught me, knowingly and unknowingly, several things. From fighting through to surviving, leaning on to hope, managing emotions, enjoying life as it is, living in the moment, and everything else, all came from her. And for that, I will always be grateful to her.

So, after I learned something terrible had happened, I found it difficult to breathe. I could feel this unexplainable sensation in my heart that grew bigger and bigger until I realized that it was grief. I was too dejected to wrap my head around the fact that someone would be horrible enough to hunt and kill an innocent animal. An animal loved throughout the valley, an animal that had only recently become a mother of twin pups, an animal as alive as a human.

I couldn't hold the rage and hate suddenly took form in my chest. And I kept thinking how humans, in general, are unkind to animals. I started sobbing at the thought that there are people with so much ignorance in their hearts that they take away the lives of poor, innocent animals.

I had many questions circling my head, all of them simple, asking a simple "why?" I couldn't comprehend anything... anything at all. All I could think about was the infinite things I had learned from my dear friend. Everywhere I looked, and everything I did reminded me of Wolf 926F. And no matter how hard I tried, I couldn't help but feel there was now a void that will never be fulfilled.

And maybe that is the thing about a situation. Because you can let go... That is the easy part. It is moving on that's painful. Everyone must pass on eventually, but you never see it coming. And even after you accept something has happened, it takes a long while for your heart to fully admit that something... something unfortunate has happened. That you are dealing with a loss from which getting past is a hassle itself.

Admission comes easily, but you take much time to learn to live without that thing. Be it a person, a thing, an animal, or even a feeling.

I knew what the course of "getting over" something was, according to Wolf 926F, but I took my due time to get past the idea that from then on, I would not be able to appreciate Wolf 926F's face, not stare in her eyes and let her wash away my pain. That from now on, I would have to continue a life without Wolf 926F, with only the lessons I learned from her, all of which are etched in my soul.

When she was taken from this earth, a piece of me was taken with her. However, what she taught me was invaluable. The foundation of survival instinct exists within us before learned experience.

Keep your eyes on the prize, not the obstacles. What we have once enjoyed, we can never lose. All that we deeply love becomes part of us.

I have healed, time heals almost everything, but that part of my grief is packed in a box and stored at the back of my head.

To this day, that scar is fresh, as if it only happened yesterday. And to this day, there is one question to which I have not yet found the answer. I don't think I ever will.

She saved my life; why couldn't I save hers?

But her legacy will always remain here in the valley of the wolves. Thank you, Wolf 926F, for all you have given me through our encounters in this valley of the wolves.

Through the wolf paw print, tattooed on the pulse of my right wrist, I know that her heart will forever beat with mine. Goodbyes are only for those who love with their eyes. Because those who love with their heart and soul, there is no separation. She will forever reign supreme over the Lamar Valley in Yellowstone National Park.

On the day I found out about her death, I felt a tidal wave of emotions consume my body. Hatred had entered my body and was ravaging my mind with impure vigilante thoughts. I didn't know where to turn; there was no rain there either. It seemed like everything that I had stood for in my life was falling apart.

I slowly walked out of my house and began to walk in a zombie-like state. I was just trying to process all that had happened. I couldn't believe it. Was my teacher gone?

I felt empty, like something inside of me had been taken out. I wanted to cry, but this time my tears wouldn't fall. Instead, I felt a fit of burning anger in my brain. Why her? Why by a bullet of a wolf-hating assassin? I kept thinking that I had significant work to do. Her story could not end this way. Because I wouldn't let it.

After 30 minutes of walking, it began to flurry.

Frozen rain.

Perfect timing. I looked up at the sky with nothing else running in my mind, besides, "I'll take it." I love rain, and it will always be my escape from everything, but at that moment, I couldn't even hope for rain. I decided to make do with what I was getting instead of rain. So, I turned to snow to bring me peace.

I kept shepherding in the snow until I arrived at my front door. As I reached there, my eyes fell to the left of the door. There, I saw a black spot on top of a days-old patch of snow. I don't know what happened or what made me do it, but I felt the urge to look closer at the spot.

As I inched forward, I realized the black spot was breathing. My eyes shot open. Immediately, worry took over me, and I drew a closer look at the spot.

Before long, I realized that the spot was a small, black kitten. And it was *frozen*. I was completely petrified, so I touched it. It was freezing, and it wasn't moving at all. I had no idea if the kitten was dead or alive, and my instincts told me that it wasn't. I quickly ran into my house and turned on the fireplace.

Now I've heard about the myth that follows, about how a black cat is a sign of bad luck. But at that moment, nothing else mattered. And believe me, while there is one side of the coin that tells you that crossing paths with a black cat brings you bad luck, the other side tells us that petting a black cat will make them loyal to you for the rest of your life.

And I was more than thrilled to be able to make a new friend.

So, I prayed to the Lord that this kitten was alive. I wanted to take care of the kitten. My mind couldn't let go of the image of that little kitten that lay like a dead, frozen being on my door. I couldn't save my teacher, but maybe I could save the baby.

For the next few hours, I sat with this frozen black kitten on my warm belly. I was helping that baby get warm. But I was helping myself. And I didn't realize it until after.

Did he know he was healing my broken heart? I kept caressing the baby, hoping he would stay alive. At dusk, he finally opened his eyes and yawned. I breathed in a sigh of relief. Now, I knew he would survive.

Once the little kitten yawned, I decided to turn all my attention to this little black kitten. I kept myself busy taking care of him. I began feeding him, got him a place to keep warm, got him a litter box and more food. During this time, my heart didn't ache, and I truly began feeling that this situation was a gift from Wolf 926F to help me cope with her loss. Nothing else made sense, and I am eternally thankful to the spirit of Wolf 926F that brought me closer to this baby.

And as usual, it worked. The cat is part of my family now. Black fur. Yellow eyes. This little soul reflects something familiar... So, I named him something close to my heart, *Sinatra.*

I thought of naming my new kitten "Sinatra" after the singer Frank Sinatra. His song, "Singing in the Rain," was the second song my grandparents would sing to me.

When I saw Wolf 926F with her pups, it was one of the most joyous moments of my life. Gazing at her, playing with her pups, made my heart bloom with love. And at that moment, I could hear the song "Singing in the Rain" playing in my head.

After that picture-perfect moment shattered from my imagination, the closest I could get to that moment was with the little black kitten I found in the snow. And I didn't recall any other name that seemed fitting more than Sinatra.

I will never understand how cruel someone could be, and how someone could live with oneself after killing an innocent animal. My brain tells me that only a cynically immoral soul could conclude he would feel better about himself by bringing so much sadness to all who knew and loved her. Wolf 926F could not have known, on that fateful day, that this impulsive, thrill-seeking, non-empathetic human premeditatively wanted to end her life.

On Saturday, November 24, 2018, two days after Thanksgiving, after being stalked on a snowy dirt road, she could not have known this wretched soul was pointing a weapon at her heart approximately fifty yards away. After all, she was used to humans holding up cameras and spotting scopes in the park, which never caused her any harm. Only this time, she was in Silvergate, barely out of the safe invisible boundary of

Yellowstone. Perhaps Montana should take a closer look at the economics of wolf hunting. They should strengthen protection for wolves who venture out of Yellowstone's invisible boundary into areas where they become targets for hunters.

I wanted to be upset at the hunter and angry at the hunting laws that allowed her death, but I could not move past grief. But grief does not define you. It reveals you.

And just like that, everything changed again.

The Gift

"There is always a silver lining after a storm." We have all heard it, but I don't think anyone believes it, just like me. But like everything else, I was proven wrong.

Do you know that some tornadoes strike rapidly? They are so unforeseen that they occur without time or even a sign for a tornado warning, and sometimes without a thunderstorm in the vicinity. When you watch a rapidly emerging tornado, it is important to know that you cannot depend on spotting a funnel. The clouds or the rain may block your view.

This is how my mind felt upon learning of the way Wolf 926F had left this world. I wanted and needed to know every detail. My mind felt like the inside of a tornado. Which, at the end of the day, is still a storm. And there is so much destruction that can be caused by storms.

About 15 years ago, when I was in Abilene, Texas, I played softball in an open field. It was sometime late in the afternoon. Suddenly, without warning, loud sirens started going off. My ears started banging, my heart began racing, and the sky turned into violent shades of swirling dark grays and blacks.

I could see all the softball players running here and there, hurrying to leave the field and get some cover. I probably should have done the same, but I just stayed there and stared eagerly to see it transform into an evil sky.

I don't know what was happening; I felt like I was almost hypnotized. I recall watching the birth of this funnel cloud right over me. Alone, I sat in the middle of the softball field, looking directly up into mother nature's wrath. Little by little, I started to feel pellets of frozen rain hit my skin.

Hail.

Maybe from growing up in the Florida Keys and living under the constant threat of hurricanes, I felt unafraid. Tornadoes are usually born from thunderstorms. It is a violently rotating column of air in contact with both the surfaces of the Earth and a cloud. These windstorms are known as a twister.

These creations of nature are known for the destruction they cause. And while for the first time that I experienced it, the damage I witnessed wasn't physical, it was contrasting the next time I had to go through it. It was more mental, psychological, and spiritual. And there was a consistent rage inside of me, with the tornado swirling in my head, heart, and eyes.

In the upcoming weeks, I gained the knowledge I needed to realize, and it was unacceptable. It appeared this wolf was targeted and killed for no other reason, except for being a wolf. Although she spent all her life in the safety of Yellowstone National Park, on this cold day in November, her life was taken by a selfish human who presumably wanted her as a trophy. Although by some accounts she was supposedly legally "harvested," the killing of this well-known wolf has drawn much outcry for greater protection of wolves directly outside the park boundary. In my attempt to say farewell, I decided to go back and visit the tree where we first met. But not before, I would visit the spot where her life was so senselessly taken. In the very spot, which still showed evidence of her ambush, I placed a stunning black crystal along with a small black wolf wearing a gold crown.

For a few moments, I laid there on that cold, dirty, snowy road. I prayed for her peace and promised I would do my best to honor her life. Wolf 926F has done a lot for me. She had not been solely my savior; she was my soulmate, my best friend, my teacher. She was everything to me, and the least I could do for her was honor her memory.

In times of fear, confusion, or uncertainty, it is susceptible to consider black crystals as negative, dark, or threatening. But, in a positive state, they can signify restful emptiness, mystery, potential, and possibility. Black crystals are often used as protective amulets. And while some people may have told me, "Not to put so much thought into it", I decided it was something I needed to do. So, I left it there in honor of her life. There is no harm in believing that some good might come out of a prevailing, supposedly sinful thought.

I wanted to do something memorable during the time I was there, so later in the day, I hiked to our special meeting tree in Round Prairie. The wind was perfect, soft, and unhurried, but cool with the sun shining in perfect complement with the air. My mind was continuously revolving around the thoughts of Wolf 926F. There was no direction of the thoughts, it was like a cloud above my head, and I didn't know how to make it stop.

As I made my way to our tree, I tripped over a broken rock in the soda butte creek. I bent over and picked it up.

I was compelled to look at it carefully. Of course, there was no way it could be an ordinary rock. I studied it carefully and realized that this broken rock looked like half of a heart. I scanned around, and that's when my eyes fell on the other half of the rock. I reached back into the creek and grabbed its other half to complete the shape it made.

I looked at the rocks in my hands. It was a perfectly broken rock, shaped like a heart, split in two. I didn't even take a moment to believe this was intentional. I instantly knew this was a gift from her, a gift of the wild. I believe this broken rock signifies the beauty of what can come from a broken heart. Hurt. Prayers. Strength. Courage. Power. Bravery. There is so much that a broken heart signifies.

But I'm sure the broken rock is a representation of the connection between two wild souls. It was a powerful moment. As I sat there in the same spot where we first met, marveling at this wondrous gift, I felt a warm sensation of air at the back of my neck. I glanced back over at our tree holding the perfectly broken heart-shaped rock, and I felt ease in my pain. I closed my eyes and let the air hover over me completely. I knew that I was not alone. Wolf 926F was with me. And nothing made me happier.

So, even after her body had left the world, I knew that our souls were still connected and would always be. Maybe that's the thing about spiritual connections, that even when you think you are alone in the world, you're not. And knowing that is the best thing in the world.

From Key West to Cooke City

I admit I am also a hunter. I hunt wolves in the park. Only, I shoot them with my camera, not a weapon. As a child growing up in Key West, I heard of Ernest Hemingway's stories of spending time out West in the Northeast corner of Yellowstone.

Ernest Hemmingway spent five summers at a ranch on the edge of Yellowstone National Park. It is no surprise that he did some of his best writings here. He had an amazing time in the mountains there, and twelve of his most famous writings relate to these mountains, including For Whom the Bell Tolls.

His favorite place to write in the world was a ranch near the small wilderness town of Cooke City, Montana, on the edge of Yellowstone, and he said so himself. He made the comparison of that ranch with Paris and Madrid.

The discovery that the infamous writer and I have shared many of the same outdoor experiences both in my hometown of Key West and my adopted town of Cooke City was fascinating. The hunter who took the life of Wolf 926F is a man from Cooke City. We are posthumously connected.

I know Cooke City well. It is like Key West in so many ways. Both these small towns are excluded from the most realistic ways of most daily lives. Key West, Florida (8 feet above sea level) and Cooke City, Montana (8,000 feet above sea level) are both the ends of the road. It is hard to explain unless you have lived there. The freedom you have is unique to boating and fishing in Key West, or snowmobiles and hunting in Cooke City. Small. Close-knit. Decadent. Free to do whatever you want, mostly without consequences.

As per my experience, I don't anticipate that there is anything in life that comes and goes without consequence. There are many factors that you must consider when you intend to make a decision. A lot that you must be careful about: and a lot that you must pay for.

During the last few days that I spent with Wolf 926F, I could feel like I was the happiest person on the planet. During the prior four years, we had both lost so much, but gained equally much. I have talked about it a million times now, but there is no way I can ever explain how much she meant to me. She still does. To say that I owe my healing to her is an understatement. I understood that she was more than just a wolf to me from the beginning; I truly wish everyone else could have too. Especially the hunter.

Maybe that was the end of the road for me. Maybe I will never have the heart to talk to that hunter and ask him in person about the rumors and mysteries surrounding that fateful day in question.

But I would like to do so. After all, I owe much to Wolf 926F, and if there is anything I can do to honor her existence, I would go to the ends of the world to do it.

She gave me a new spirit; she helped me cope; she helped me understand, develop, and evolve. She gave me a new direction in life, she gave me a gift, and she gave me Sinatra. I want to give her something in return, and the best thing I could give her is love and honor. For everything she has done for me in the last few years of her life.

I'm aware of where the hunter lives and works. For a complicated period, I used to think that the hunter was some immoral human being with no values. Someone, who was a monster, someone who did not have any feelings or emotions himself? I don't know if that is true, but to this day, I have not denied this theory of mine.

But I also know that, like me, the hunter has isolated himself in a small town. A place where he has sheltered himself from the rest of the world.

I often think, what if the hunter is not all that different from me. Maybe, he is a woeful man looking for diversions and distractions. Maybe he feels like he is at the bottom of the totem pole in his life.

What if this was an attempt by the hunter to be noticed? Maybe I should contact him and ask him to meet me face to face. I have so many questions beyond the why. I want to know what he was thinking at the point when he decided to shoot. At that moment, he decided to fire the bullet, what was the thing that crossed his mind? How could he be so disturbed by something that he decided to let his frustration out on a creature, an innocent creature, who spent her life sacrificing everything?

But what if... What if he wants to be forgiven for all of it? Because what if his hatred for wolves stems from a much larger event? Maybe, just maybe, he wants to be forgiven after all the backlash he has endured for taking her life.

Will he grant me the privilege of bringing her home? To place her earthly remains back where she belongs, into the wild? Or what about a place where she can be celebrated by all the humans who knew and loved her?

I often wonder if I can ever give Wolf 926F something of equal value she has gifted me. My best friend, my teacher, my soulmate... Wolf 926F gave me the gift of the wild. I want to reciprocate it, and the only way I can do so is by exchanging a gift with the hunter.

What if the hunter is looking for forgiveness? And if he is, I can humbly ask him to allow me his trophy, my friend Wolf 926F, in return for forgiveness. Not just for me, but for everyone else, everyone who has been touched and has come to love Wolf 926F. This would be a gift shared worldwide. If I can exchange gifts with the hunter, I can give Wolf 926F her due honor, as I will be able to place her remains on the earth, from where she was born, grew up, lived, gave life, loved, and lost. I will return her into the wild, her home. To give her back the gift she once gave me.

This would be an unlikely friendship and an exchange of gifts—forgiveness for bringing her home.

But for this to happen, the hunter must agree with my theory. And maybe... maybe this book will help the hunter change his heart about everything that happened. And then, the true hero of this story will be him, and him alone. But, has the novelty of killing her worn off?

My wanderlust goes on. I often ask myself, "What would Wolf 926F do?" I know, undoubtedly, exactly what she would do. She would form that unlikely friendship. Something that she had mastered in the valley of the wolves.

I remember during one time in her life, she and her mate were ambushed. Another rival wolf pack had charged and killed her much-beloved mate, Wolf 925M. Unfortunately, she was vulnerable during this time, as she was expecting her pups. Her mate, Wolf 925M, died a hero as he gave his life to save his mate and his future pups. However, she was now faced with the harsh reality that her pups would likely not survive. But Wolf 926F was never exactly an ordinary wolf. Instead of letting nature take its course, she foresaw it would be best to befriend those rival wolves who had just killed her mate. She needed them.

She single-mindedly decided to allow these dispersers from the enemy pack to join her territory to help her raise her pups. Against all odds, she formed that unlikely friendship with the known combatants and came out a winner.

The most important lesson I have learned in my time with the wolves is loyalty. A wolf pack is an exceedingly complex social unit. It is an extended family of a mate, parents, offspring, siblings, aunts, uncles, and sometimes dispersers from an outside pack. Wolves instinctively know what it means to be a loyal pack member. Throughout their lives, they remain fiercely loyal to their pack and are the ultimate team players. A wolf pack that does not work together, as one will not survive. Wolves will do anything to protect their mates, their family, and their loved ones. This includes even giving up their own lives if they must. The wolf always remains loyal, come what may, and he trusts his pack mates to do the same. Working together benefits the pack. Wolves know there is no place in life for selfishness when you are part of a team. These instinctual rules are for every individual's best, including his own, so he follows them throughout his existence.

When I think about it, these wolves have truly instilled loyalty in my heart. I would be deflecting from the values she has passed down to me in the time I have spent with her.

If I don't convince my heart to befriend the hunter, I will never honor my friend in her true spirit.

I'm out here, searching for answers. I dream a lot as an adult. And that is the start of everything. The start of a new chapter. The start of a new journey.

The start of a new me. And I am ready. Welcome to the end of the road. But is it the end?

Epilogue

926F was born into the Lamar Canyon pack in April 2011. She is the daughter of alphas '06 Female (832F) and 755M. Anchoring their territory once again in Lamar Valley, the Lamar pack, like their predecessors (the Druid Peak pack), became a marquee attraction in the park. Her parents had five pups, all of which survived that year. In 2012, 926F survived many challenges, setting the stage for the strong female 926F would become. The first challenge she faced was when the Mollie's pack overran their den site; an event that all the 2012 pups survived due to her mother's leadership. The second would alter her life dramatically when her mother, the '06 Female, and her uncle, beta male

754M, were killed during the wolf-hunting season east of the park in Wyoming. Her father, 755M, dispersed from the pack soon after because he was also the father of all ten-pack members and unlikely to breed with them. This left 926b and her siblings on their own. Her older sister 776F claimed the role of the alpha female, but she and many of the remaining pack members eventually settled in the Wyoming area, not far from where her mother had been killed. 926F had other plans, and in 2013 she and her older sister Middle Gray left their siblings to return to their natal territory in Lamar Valley. They settled in with a new male known as Big Gray at the time, 925M (a Pahaska pack wolf from outside and east of the park in Wyoming), and the two sisters quickly became rivals for his attention. The pack had two pups that year, likely born to Middle Gray, but none of them survived. Middle Gray disappeared in November 2013, and 926F and 925M became a new alpha pair. In 2014, they went on to produce a litter of seven pups, of which six lived through the end of the year. In early 2015, life would throw 926F yet another curveball when she and her pack (six eleven-month-old pups and her mate 925M) traveled into enemy territory looking for better hunting opportunities than could be found in Lamar Valley that winter. They traveled to the west and successfully killed an elk, providing much-needed nutrients to the six youngsters. However, on their way back to the Lamar Valley, the entire pack was caught at unawares by the Prospect Peak pack near the Slough Creek area. Her mate 925M bravely stood his ground, allowing a very pregnant 926F and the six pups to escape. The focus of the Prospect attack became 925g, with as many as 12 wolves surrounding and biting him. 926F's sons, Little Gray and 967M turned back to help their besieged father. Little Gray was the first to charge down the hill to the scene of the attack and draw several Prospect wolves to chase after him. Then came 967M, charging down the hill and drawing several more Prospects after him. One Prospect pup was left at the scene of the attack, and even though severely wounded, 925M was able to scare off the remaining Prospect pup. 926F's alpha mate then limped away from the attack scene to the cover of deep sagebrush nearby. He would eventually die from his wounds. Evidence exists to indicate that 926F, followed by her pups, would eventually make it back to the side of her dying alpha mate, revealing the depth of a pair-bond so strong that not even the danger of an enemy pack could keep her away. 926F was now left with six mouths to feed and new pups on the way. There were now no experienced adult hunters to provide for her in the next coming months. But, in a strange twist of events, four males from the Prospects showed up in her territory, the same males who were likely responsible for the death of her mate. Having nowhere to run, 926F decided the only chance she would have to protect her family would be to win over these invading boys. She sent the eleven-month-old pups off into the woods while she stood her ground. As the stand-still proceeded, she eventually began to wag her tail at the boys, winning them over in the end. The four Prospect males became new members of the Lamar Canyon pack. A wolf named Twin (992M) settled into the role of alpha male, and 926F had found not only one male to help care for her and her pups who would soon arrive but had three other experienced new pack members as well. She gave birth to five pups that year. Three of the pups survived, but by the end of 2015, many of the pack members had varying degrees of mange infection. She has since survived repeated upheavals to her pack. By the end of 2016, three of the four males who had joined her, including her mate Twin (992M), would be dead. One of the males, 965M, was often seen with her, but he bounced back and forth between the Lamars and the Prospects, making for an unreliable pack member. 965M found himself outside of the protection of the park boundary, and he too was dead by December 2016. 926F and her daughter Little-T have since been joined by two males from the Beartooth pack from outside and northeast of the park. One of those males, 949M, became the alpha male, and his brother Small Dot became the beta male. Both females tied with 949M during the 2017 breeding season, and both females showed signs of pregnancy, but no pups appear to have survived in 2017. The larger Junction Butte pack of eight wolves took over most of Lamar Valley in 2017, and 926F and her three packmates were forced to the northeastern edges of their territory. Then her mate 949M showed signs of some sort of trauma for ten days in August. From August 14-24, he remained near a bison carcass at The Confluence and was clearly suffering from some kind of disease or head injury. He died on August 24, 2017, and his body was retrieved on August 25 for examination. The result of the examination determined that his cause of death was canine distemper, which may have also been the cause of the death for the pack's April 2017 litters (as well as the pup litters of at least two other packs. The loss of 949M represents the third alpha mate 926F has lost (925M/Big Gray, 992M/Twin, and 949M) since she assumed alpha leadership of the Lamar Canyon pack in 2013. By the end of 2017, 926F was submitting to her daughter, Little-T, and Small Dot had assumed the role of the alpha male. In April 2018, both Lamar Canyon females exhibited signs of pregnancy, but the pack had become increasingly elusive and hard to see that year. A black pup or two was seen in the company of the three adults occasionally until mid-day, October 26, 2018, when two guides of Yellowstone Wolf Tracker discovered eight black wolves in Soda Butte Canyon. It was the 926F, Little-T, Small Dot, and five black pups! It was a joyous moment for all because it meant the long-awaited revitalization of the Lamar Canyon Pack, an all-black wolf pack! But the joy was short-lived. The larger Junction Butte Pack with eight adult wolves had taken over most of Lamar Valley, and the smaller Lamar Canyon Pack with only three adult wolves was pushed to the extreme northeast corner of their territory. The Lamars became increasingly reclusive among the thick trees of the northeast corner of Yellowstone National Park, with only 926 herself mostly seen. Later that year, the pack began traveling outside the park's boundary and among the gateway communities of Silver Gate and Cooke City in

Montana. Then on November 24, 2018, the pack's matriarch, 926F, was shot and killed only a mile outside the park's boundary during Montana's wolf hunting season. It was ruled a legal shooting by Montana Fish Wildlife & Parks, but many questions and concerns were raised, and the death of this famous wolf so near the park boundary made news across the world. It was almost six years to the date earlier that her famous mother and founding alpha of the Lamar Canyon Pack, the '06 Female, was shot (December 6, 2012). 926F's life was filled with triumphs and tragedies, and as wolf researcher Rick McIntyre reminds us, "In Memory of Yellowstone Wolf 926F ... There are many other stories to tell of 926, but the ones I just related give you a sense of what she was like. She had a long, exciting life and overcame great difficulties. Tens of thousands of people got to see her live that life and were inspired by her grit and determination. Her family is carrying on. Next April, her adult daughter will likely have a litter of new pups at the pack's den." On

October 5, 2019, Little T was spotted with a black yearling and two black pups!

The legacy of 926 lives on!

- by Yellowstone Wolf Genealogy

The Yellowstone Wolf Family Tree is Ancestry.com's largest and most unique family tree, with over 600 human guests and featuring the life stories and genealogy of over 1,200 Yellowstone wolves! To join the hundreds and become a free guest of the tree, go to the webportal www.wolfgenes.info and select the Ancestry. From there, scroll down to the invitation section and follow the instructions to submit your guest request.
- Leo Leckie

Saving Tadpoles

The First Time

The Last Time

My Gift To Her

Her Gift To Me

Warden Daily/Monthly Activity Report

Report Parameters:

Warden: Start Date: 11/27/2018 End Data: 11/27/2018

Activity Log:

Record Type	Officer Rank	Start Date	End Date	Total Actrvity HH.MM	Total Patrol HH.MM	Total Miles	Complete	Completed Date Time
	FWPWARDEN	11/27/2018 8 30:00 AM	11/27/2018 6:00:00 PM	6.30	3.00	0	Tru01	11/27/2018 6:00:02 PM

Activity Log Detail:

Date	Slart Date	Encl Date	HH.MM	Group Desc	Code Oesc	Description	Location	••••
11/27/2018	11/27/2018 3 30:00 PM	11/27/2018 4 30:00 PM	1.00	CRIMINAL INVESTIGATION	WILDLIFE	Self turn in. Mule deer harvested afte, season closure in HD313. Hunter cited and deer seil.cd. CAD8300.	ROYAL TETON RANCH	
	11/27/2018 8 37:00 AM	11/27/2018 8 37:00 AM	0.00	WARDEN PATROL NOTE	NULL	Phone calls. Emails.	OFFICE	0
	11/27/2018 10:00:00AM	11/27/2018 3 30:00PM	5.30	PRACTMTY	PR URBAN WILDLIFE –OTHER	Tr.wel lo Cooke City to check in a wol7 legally harvested in HD316. Cites #MTW0000909. Took pics & lolwardad to wolf biologist.	COOKE CITY	0

ENFORCEMENT DIVISION
Region 3 Case Report

1400 S. 19th
Bozeman, MT 59718
(406)-224-5207

CAD Number.
FWP18CAD008447

Date of Report
1216/2018

Location:
Silver Gate, MT

Distribution of Copies:

Incident Type:
Legal Wolf Harvest

Oate(s) Occurred:
11/24/2018

MCA Offense(s):
None

Person(s) Involved:
Choose an item.

1. —— unter)

    008/ALS: ——

    contact Number:Click or tap here to enter text.

Witness

2.

    Address:

    008/ALS:

    Contact Number:

Narrative:

Monday, November 26th, 2018, at approximately 1432 hours I received a voicemail via cell phone from a hunter in the Cooke City, MT area who advised he had harvested a wolf and requested I meet with him to inspect the animal as required per current Montana hunting regulations. I contacted him a short time later and arranged to meet him the following day at his residence in Cooke City.

- I arrived at the hunter's residence at approximately 1230 hrs on 11/27/18.
- I observed a tracked ATV backed up to the garage door with blood in the bed and in the snow beneath it. I entered the garage and saw a wolf hide on a saw horse next to a skinned carcass hanging from an overhead beam with a bright yellow carcass tag affixed to a leg. I removed the tag to inspect it and found it to be properly validated as required.
- I inspected the hide, skull, and carcass and all appeared to be in order. The hunter indicated he had killed the wolf at approx. 1430 hours on Saturday, 11/24/18. He then called the 1-800 reporting line and was issued Ref. #GW-181125-101. I completed a wolf harvest form and installed CITES pelt tag #MTW0000909 through the pelt ensuring it was securely fastened.
- The hunter stated it was well known throughout the area that a pack of wolves had been frequenting this location for several days attempting to kill one of 3 moose wintering there.
- News of the wolves had drawn quite a few hunters to the area and the hunter said he knew of at least 10 local residents actively pursuing them.
- The hunter said he left work early and drove to the area on his tracked ATV to hunt the wolves. He said he was wearing hunter orange and had his 223 caliber rifle in the rack next to him.
- The hunter drove to private property where he has standing permission for access and parked his ATV. He exited the ATV with his rifle and walked several yards into a stand of trees and stopped. While standing there he heard a commotion a short distance in front of him and a wolf suddenly appeared in a clearing approx. 100 yds away on the same private property. He fired a single shot and the wolf jumped and turned around and raced back in the direction it had come from. The hunter returned to his ATV and started driving down the road in the direction the wolf had gone. He drove approx. 200 yds and observed the wolf dead on the road in front of him. Note: The "road" in question is a Forest Service route known as the Bannack Trail. He then validated and affixed his tag to the carcass, loaded it into his ATV, and returned to his residence.
- I responded to the location the hunter provided and observed ATV tracks which stopped at the edge of the treed property as described. I also observed human boot prints leaving the ATV towards the trees and subsequently returning. The foot prints were oriented in a north or slightly northeasterly direction indicating that if a shot was fired it was fired in a safe direction and well away from the roadway. I then walked into the clearing and observed very faint tracks in the snow possibly made by a wolf but impossible to confirm. Due to several inches of new snow, human footprints on top of the animal tracks, snowmobile traffic, and bison activity, it was impossible to follow the animal's tracks beyond just a few feet. However, I did locate the site described by the hunter where he found the dead wolf. There was a large blood spot in the snow and significant bird activity on it. Ski and snowmobile tracks had obscured all original activity. I attempted to follow the wolf's tracks backward but once again the new snow and large number of other tracks, both human and animal, prevented me from being able to do so.

⊠   Several pictures and videos submitted by concerned individuals have thus far corroborated the information provided by the hunter and my own observations. There are no additional leads at this time.   End of initial report.

Evidence Items:

Attachments:

Warden–Gardiner District | R3

Montana Fish, Wildlife & Parks

Talking points on Wolf 926F, harvested legally in WMU 316 on Nov. 24.

#926F was a 7.5-year-old black female wolf was legally hunted in WMU 316 near Cooke City.

This wolf is known to wolf researchers as wolf# 926F. She was collared and recently her collar dropped off (still identifiable by the distinct pelt).

She was part of the Lamar Canyon pack that spent the majority of their time in Yellowstone NP.

WMU 316 has a 2-wolf quota. This was the first wolf harvested in the unit this hunting season. The quota in WMU 313 has been met and hunting is closed in that unit.

The quota of two wolves in each WMU 313 and 316 is a compromise between the interests of hunters who would like to see more opportunities to hunt wolves and interests in protecting wolves for tourism and research.

#926F and members of her pack showed signs of habituation and were close to Cooke City. The main advice to the public in regards to this pack is to keep domestic dogs close by, on leash and in sight, particularly at night. Never feed wildlife, and where possible remove attractants that are close to buildings and human activity (e.g. bone piles, dumps).

Any member of the public can kill a wolf if it is in the act of attacking humans, dogs or livestock.

Even though these wolves showed signs of habituation, this hunt was still a fair chase and legal hunt. Always report signs of habituated wildlife to the appropriate authorities. This wolf was shot close to homes in Silvergate and Cooke City. This is legal as Cooke City/ Silvergate are not incorporated towns, and the wolf was not shot from the road or in a way that endangered people.

A game warden checked in the wolf and deemed that the hunt was conducted in compliance with our wolf regulations.

General wolf management points

- Montana is in the midst of its ninth season of wolf hunting. Biologists estimate Montana's wolf population to be about 850 animals, which are widely distributed in the state. This includes a minimum of 124 packs and 63 breeding pairs.
- FWP is committed to maintaining wolves on the wild landscape of Montana.
- Wolf hunting was recommended as a management tool in the 2004 Montana Wolf Conservation and Management Plan. In 2017, hunters and trappers harvested 233 wolves. Sales of license year 2017/18 wolf hunting licenses generated $380,261 for wolf management in Montana. Decisions regarding wolf hunting regulations and quotas occur on a biennial basis, with the next opportunity for public comment and engagement during the season setting meetings in the winter of 2020.

Made in the USA
Las Vegas, NV
15 January 2023

65632809R00085